T. S. Eliot

by

M. C. BRADBROOK

Published for the British Council
and the National Book League
by Longmans, Green & Co.

Three shillings and sixpence net

T. S. Eliot, although born and educated in the United States, lived in England from 1914 onwards and became a British subject in 1927. His early poetry, from 'Prufrock' to 'The Waste Land', was regarded as revolutionary and indecorous, but gradually he was accepted as a major poet by even the most conservative men of letters. His last great poetic sequence, *Four Quartets*, was completed in 1942, and henceforth, apart from minor, occasional poems, he devoted himself to dramatic verse, winning a wide audience for his three post-war plays. Eliot's criticism exerted a powerful influence for over four decades, and there was a constant interplay between his critical and his creative work. The awards of the Nobel Prize for Literature, the American Medal of Freedom and the British Order of Merit were tributes to his fame in the world at large, his native land and the country which he honoured by his act of adoption.

Miss Bradbrook is Professor in English Literature at Cambridge, and from October 1968 Mistress of Girton College by pre-election. She has published studies of such diverse figures as Marvell, Ibsen and Conrad; and is best known for her work on the Elizabethan Theatre. Among her most recent publications are *Shakespeare and Elizabethan Poetry* (1951), *The Growth and Structure of Elizabethan Comedy* (1955), *The Rise of the Common Player* (1962) and *English Dramatic Form* (1965).

Bibliographical Series
of Supplements to 'British Book News'
on Writers and Their Work

★

GENERAL EDITOR
Geoffrey Bullough

T. S. ELIOT

T. S. ELIOT

by

M. C. BRADBROOK

PUBLISHED FOR
THE BRITISH COUNCIL
AND THE NATIONAL BOOK LEAGUE
BY LONGMANS, GREEN & CO

LONGMANS, GREEN & CO LTD
48 Grosvenor Street, London, W1

*Associated companies, branches and
representatives throughout the world*

*First published 1950
Revised editions, 1951, 1955, 1958, 1960, 1963, 1965
Reprinted with minor amendments to text
and additions to bibliography 1968*
© Muriel Bradbrook, 1960, 1963, 1965

*Printed in Great Britain by
F. Mildner & Sons, London, EC1*

CONTENTS

¶ T. S. Eliot was born at St Louis, Missouri, on 26 September 1888. He died in London on 4 January 1965.

T. S. ELIOT

I. INTRODUCTORY

WHEN, on 26 September 1948, T. S. Eliot celebrated his sixtieth birthday, tributes which he received from the country of his birth and the country of his adoption, from Europe, and indeed from all over the world made it plain that he was very generally acknowledged as the greatest living poet of the English language. Nevertheless, his poetry at first provoked strong disagreement, and the reviews of his later work, especially his dramas, show that his continued development and intellectual growth could still give rise to new misunderstanding.

Eliot's literary career illustrates in a striking manner the controlling force of the poetic impulse. He was born in St Louis, Missouri, U.S.A., a large industrial city, where his father held an important position in the business world. But he was descended on both sides from New England families of the early settlements: his ancestor, Andrew Eliot, went to Massachusetts from the Somerset village of East Coker in 1670, and his mother was a descendant of Isaac Stearns, who went out in 1630 as one of the original settlers of the Massachusetts Bay Colony. Among his forebears T. S. Eliot numbered many distinguished scholars, clergymen, and men of letters; in his early poems there are a number of sketches, not always entirely dutiful, of Boston relatives and of that little society, Puritan, earnestly intellectual, and highly exclusive, which survived as the aristocracy of America until quite recently, and which still in some measure survives, although it no longer centres upon the city of Boston. In *Four Quartets*, Eliot has described both East Coker, the village from which his family emigrated nearly three hundred years ago, and, in 'The Dry Salvages', the Massachusetts coast which he knew in his childhood.

Eliot's family tradition connected him with Harvard, where he received his education. At Harvard there is now a collection of material relating to Eliot's early life, together with much of his *juvenilia*. He spent four years at this most famous university, being especially interested in the study of philosophy. In 1910 he went to the Sorbonne, to read literature and philosophy, subsequently returning to Harvard for further study. Afterwards he studied in Germany and at Oxford. During the war of 1914–18 he stayed in England, working first a schoolmaster, then as a banker, and finally as an editor and publisher. It was during this period that his poetic work began to appear in various magazines, and between 1917 and 1920 in small volumes. But it was in 1922, with the publication of 'The Waste Land', that Eliot assumed that commanding position in English poetry which he ever after retained. In 1927 he became a British subject, and announced in the preface to a book of essays that he was now a classicist in literature, a royalist in politics and an Anglo-Catholic in religion, a statement which caused some disturbance in literary circles, where none of these tenets was very prominently advocated.

During the next decade he published some important poetry, wrote and lectured on a wide variety of subjects connected with literature and society and, through his editing of the *Criterion*, a quarterly magazine, exercised considerable influence upon the literary world. After the war he published what many people consider his greatest poem, *Four Quartets*, then turned quite deliberately to the stage; but the *Criterion* ceased publication in 1939, and Eliot tended to write less criticism than formerly. His authority and reputation had, however, grown steadily, and whilst in the nineteen-twenties he was known chiefly to the young and enthusiastic students of the universities and to the younger literary generation in London, he became gradually accepted during the course of the next decade by the more traditional and conservative guardians of literary reputations. He is now treated with the greatest respect by even the crustier old gentlemen of the clubs and High Tables, and accorded the reverence (which he would have found somewhat embarrassing) of literary ladies and provincial clerics. He received from King George VI the Order of Merit, that most rare and coveted of honours, the Nobel Prize for Literature in 1948 and the highest American civilian honour, the Medal of Freedom, in 1964. His double task has been the interpretation of the age to itself, 'holding the Mirror up to Nature' as the greatest poet of all proclaimed, and maintaining the standards of strict literary excellence, 'purifying the dialect of the tribe', as he himself, quoting Mallarmé, declared his aim to be. As Eliot has said of another poet, in his own work the reader will find 'a record of the spiritual struggles of a man of intellectual power and emotional intensity who gave much toil to perfecting his verses. As such, it should be a document of interest to all who are curious to understand their fellow men.'

II. THE POET OF 'THE WASTE LAND'

Eliot's early poetry, published during the war of 1914–18, depicts in ironic and epigrammatic terseness the little anxieties, social embarrassments, and unacknowledged vacuity of polite society in Boston and London. The world he displays is the world of Henry James's novels, where frustrated society ladies breathe their invitations and deprecations by a faint nuance, where corrupt financiers and decayed nobility drive their social bargains, where the final reckoning discloses only that

> I have measured out my life with coffee spoons.

In his collection of essays, *Abinger Harvest*, E. M. Forster has described the relief with which he discovered a little volume of Eliot during a period of convalescence in Cairo:

For what, in that world of gigantic horror, was tolerable except the slight gestures of dissent? He who measured himself against the war, who drew himself to his full height, as it were, and said to Armadillo-Armageddon 'Avaunt!' collapsed at once into a pinch of dust. But he who could turn aside to complain of ladies and drawing rooms preserved a tiny drop of our self-respect, he carried on the human heritage.

Yet behind the hesitancies, the ironic wit of a young man trying to protect himself against *faux pas* in the society of the Old World, behind the futilities and the boredom of the middle-aged unsuccessful Prufrock, or the middle-aged unsuccessful lady of 'Portrait of a Lady', with its reminiscence of Henry James in the very title, Eliot would occasionally show a glimpse of horror or of glory. In a single phrase—joined with some sardonic self-depreciatory gesture—he can call up a vision of lyric beauty, alien but poignantly felt. This very simple device, the juxtaposition of the lovely and the squalid, or the passionate and the trivial, so that they make their own comment on one another, is the basis of his poetic structure:

> I grow old . . . I grow old . . .
> I shall wear the bottoms of my trousers rolled.
> Shall I part my hair behind? Do I dare to eat a peach?
> I shall wear white flannel trousers, and walk upon the beach.
> I have heard the mermaids singing, each to each.
>
> I do not think that they will sing to me.
>
> I have seen them riding seaward on the waves
> Combing the white hair of the waves blown back
> When the wind blows the waters white and black.
>
> We have lingered in the chambers of the sea
> By seagirls wreathed with seaweed red and brown
> Till human voices wake us, and we drown.

Here are not only echoes of Keats's 'magic casements opening on the foam Of perilous seas', of the chambers of the sea where the forsaken Merman of Arnold lingered—the situation, it will be noted, is reversed—but the fresh stiff drive of a lively off-shore breeze. This seascape may be compared with those of 'Mr Apollinax' and 'Gerontion', 'Marina', the last poem of 'Ash Wednesday', and 'The Dry Salvages' (the third of *Four Quartets*). Eliot has a few strong and central symbols, as he has a few strong and central themes, and the sea as the source of primal life and energy is one of the most important. Hence even in the lovely fourth movement of 'The Waste Land', 'Death by Water'—a passage adapted from the French of his poem, 'Dans le Restaurant'—Phlebas, the drowned Phoenician sailor, appears as one who has lived a full simple natural life and died a clean death. In the land of drought, Death by Water holds more beauty than terror; for both the present scene and the recollections are of beauty:

> Gentile or Jew,
> O you who turn the wheel and look to windward,
> Consider Phlebas, who was once handsome and tall as you.

To the generation which wasted its youth in that earlier war, the shock of discovering the instability of their world was more severe than anything which the generation of 1939 had to meet. Political and religious scepticism, already an intellectual fashion, was strengthened by general disillusion, and the temper in England during the war years and the following decade was one of cynicism, irony, and a protective, defensive toughness of mind. Housman, Lytton Strachey, Aldous Huxley, and the Sitwells were the fashionable reading of the intellectuals: the poetry of Donne and other difficult seventeenth-century poets enjoyed a vogue which was partly created by the critical writings of Eliot himself (see below, p. 52). Social conventions were by general consent taboo: and while it could be considered by serious critics a virtue in Eliot to achieve 'a complete severance between his poetry and *all* beliefs', it was held that experience should be as wide, unrestricted and uninhibited as possible. The juvenile naughtiness of the neurotic 'twenties takes on in retrospect a certain pathos. It was the reaction from a shattering experience, and the refuge of those who did not wish to remember because they could not attempt to organize or control their memories of the war years. Eliot's early poetry, with its subtle deflation of feelings ('Conversation Galante'), its shocking juxtapositions in the manner of Donne ('Whispers of Immortality' and 'Mr Eliot's Sunday Morning Service') is summed up in the Sweeney poems, 'Sweeney Erect' and 'Sweeney Among the Nightingales'. The lovely world of Renaissance art, classic legend, and natural beauty is superimposed upon the squalors of tavern and brothel. There is no comment, no explanation and no attempt to connect the two. Instead the sharp hard lines of the verse, the alternation of magnificence and familiarity in the words and the startling incongruity of the images are left to make their own effect. The reader has to complete the work within his own experience. Here are to be seen two of Eliot's principal poetic weapons—his use of *implication*, of statements which carry a weight far beyond their ostensive meaning which 're-echo, thus, in your mind' and which therefore oblige the reader to a peculiarly active and strenuous *participation* in the poetry. For Eliot always wrote with a very strong sense of his readers. He made demands upon them, without which the poems are incomplete. It is no use approaching Eliot in a state of wise passiveness. You have to use your wits.

This method of ironic implication is clearly of the greatest value in an age when there are in fact no longer any generally accepted standards of belief which the poet may take for granted. It enables the poet to escape or evade the kind of direct statement with which his reader may not agree—and which the poet himself will not feel capable of providing. For Eliot never claimed to speak with authority, as his later admirers suggest. He declared that some of his earlier essays

in spite of, and partly because of, their defects preserve in cryptogram certain notions which, if expressed directly would be destined to immediate obloquy, followed by perpetual oblivion.

In this ironic disclaimer may be read something of the difficulties which the contemporary climate of opinion imposed on a lyric poet. The Sweeney poems are in a sense poems in cryptogram, but each reader is invited to provide his own solution. This does not mean that they are ambiguous. They are merely condensed. The single scene, the grand vista opened by an evocative phrase, the impartial and controlled movement of the verse impose a direction even while they decline to state it:

> Gloomy Orion and the Dog
> Are veiled; and hushed the shrunken seas;
> The person in the Spanish cape
> Tries to sit on Sweeney's knees.
>
> Slips and pulls the table cloth
> Overturns a coffee cup. . . .
>
> The host with someone indistinct
> Converses at the door apart,
> The nightingales are singing near
> The Convent of the Sacred Heart,
>
> And sang within the bloody wood,
> When Agamemnon cried aloud,
> And let their liquid siftings fall
> To stain the stiff dishonoured shroud.

The lovely song and the birds' droppings, the squalid intrigue in the tavern and the murder of a King are not merely contrasted in ironic equivalence. They are somehow seen as having at least so necessary a relation as to be inseparable. Here is the source of the gratitude his contemporaries feel towards Eliot. He has interpreted the chaos of their world, so that it no longer presents itself as chaotic:

> *Erhebung* without motion, concentration
> Without elimination, both a new world
> And the old made explicit, understood
> In the completion of its partial ecstasy
> The resolution of its partial horror.
>
> 'Burnt Norton', II

Whilst the Sweeney poems sum up Eliot's achievement at this time, there are two others which point forward to his later work. These are 'La Figlia che Piange' and 'Gerontion'. It has been said, on good authority, that *La Figlia che Piange* is written about a statue of a weeping girl, which the poet hoped to see in Italy but never located. Even the word of Eliot himself would not convince me that a poem beginning

> Stand on the highest pavement of the stair—
> Lean on a garden urn—
> Weave, weave the sunlight in your hair—
> Clasp your flowers to you with a pained surprise—
> Fling them to the ground and turn
> With a fugitive resentment in your eyes:
> But weave, weave the sunlight in your hair.

had very much to do with marble. The curious shifts between second and third person in the address, the hint of a Henry James situation at the end of the second stanza, and the summing up, 'I should have lost a gesture and a pose', indicate clearly that the very substance of the poem is the relation between life and art—particularly between those moments when life falls into the ordered pattern of art; but the beautiful movement, the alternation of longing and control, conveys most poignantly a human situation which re-echoes through all the poetry down to *The Family Reunion*. 'Gerontion', 'the old man', whose soliloquy stands at the head of the *Poems* of 1920, is a dramatic figure not unlike Tiresias, the old blind seer of 'The Waste Land'. Both are voices rather than persons—the voices of representative Man, as he contemplates a decaying civilization and the pitiable fragments of humanity that inhabit this 'decayed house'. Mr Silvero, Hakagawa, Madame de Tornquist, and Fraulein von Kulp are only names, but the mixture of nationalities, the suggestions of various kinds of international hocus-pocus, artistic, or occult, picks up the description of the 'owner of the house', the Jew

> Spawned in some estaminet of Antwerp,
> Blistered in Brussels, patched and peeled in London.

All, including Gerontion, are displaced, homeless persons, whose spiritual desolation is symbolized in the traditional religious metaphor of drought. There is no apparent sequence of thought or logical arrangement in the poem, only the broken fragmentary recollections and meditations of the old man, as he recalls those heroic deaths in battle, suggestive of Homeric war, which he did not share:

> I was neither at the hot gates
> Nor fought in the warm rain
> Nor knee deep in the salt marsh, heaving a cutlass,
> Bitten by flies, fought.

In the meditation which follows, not only contemporary society, but the inner world of the individual is seen to be crumbling:

> These with a thousand small deliberations
> Protract the profit of their chill delirium,
> Excite the membrane, when the sense has cooled,
> With pungent sauces, multiply variety
> In a wilderness of mirrors.

By a technique not unlike that of the early Russian films, Eliot gives a series of 'shots' which when put together do form a single sequence. The unity lies in the mood and tone, the flat listless accents of the old man whose vision may have the inconsequence of a dream, because, as Eliot says in the quotation from Shakespeare which heads the poem,

> Thou hast nor youth nor age,
> But as it were an after dinner sleep,
> Dreaming of both.

The poem is full of echoes of Shakespeare and of other Elizabethan dramatists. These literary echoes have often caused apprehension in the mind of readers, who feel that without an ability to recognize such allusions, they may lose the point of the poem. This fear is, I think, without foundation. A successful poem does not rely upon anything but itself for the essential core of its meaning. Eliot's use of literary allusions is part of his technique of implication. As in the Sweeney poem he could evoke the majesty of Greek tragedy in the images of Agamemnon and the nightingales, could summon up a whole train of associations in contrast to what the rest of the poem suggested, so, in his many echoes of the French symbolists, Donne and the metaphysical poets, Dante and the poets of the *dolce stil nuovo*, which occur throughout 'The Waste Land', he sets his vision of desolation and spiritual drought in implicit contrast with the visionary worlds of the elder poets, his masters. Sometimes the contrasts are ironic, as the echoes of Shakespeare's *Antony and Cleopatra* in the second movement of 'The Waste Land', which describes the boudoir of a neurotic fine lady of the present day, and her rasping quarrel with an almost silent figure, her husband or her lover. Sometimes literature consoles and supports by reminding a distraught generation that it is not alone—in recognizing the right words for the present situations, it marks the first step towards control; to accept such a definition in terms of another time and another place marks also the first step towards integration. Eliot used the words of the *Inferno* to describe the city crowd that 'flowed up the hill and down King William Street' because only a Dante could define for him the depth of their desolation. The poet accepts the personal suffering which such a vision entails, and the two utterances which give it most clearly are the cry of Arnaut Daniel from his purgatorial flames 'Sovegna vos' (which is not uttered but recalled):

> Poi s'ascose nel foco che gli affina

and St. Augustine on the drowned Phoenician sailor. Each marks a renunciation, and each had echoes through Eliot's poetry for some time. There are indeed many familiar figures who appear momentarily—the old German princess; the damp and depressed figure of Lil, as described in the public-house scene; the typist, who might have been one of Sweeney's girl-friends, the three Thames-daughters, her sisters: Mme Sosostris the famous clairvoyante, and Mr Eugenides the Smyrna merchant. All are seen through the blind eyes of old Tiresias, the seer, who has 'foresuffered all'; for as Eliot explicitly says: 'The poem is what he sees.' The lesser characters are not clearly distinguished; they melt into each other, for they are phantoms inhabiting an unreal city. Such is Eliot's vision of the post-war world, a land by no means fit for heroes to live in, and which in any case most of his friends did not live to inhabit. It is a cosmic vision, seen on a small scale. Whilst Joyce took seven hundred pages to describe a single day in the life of Dublin, Eliot concentrated his vision in four hundred lines. The whole poem, but especially its last lines, employs the technique of ironic juxta-position, which has already been described, in a deeper and more tragic manner. The 'wild and whirling words' of a mind unstrung, clutching desperately at the fragmentary and disintegrating remains of the world of literature, shored against its ruin, are suddenly broken in upon by the tolling magnificence of the Sanscrit benediction:

> Datta. Dayadhvam. Damyata.
> Shantih shantih shantih

The contemporary public were of course bewildered by 'The Waste Land', but after fully forty years of exposition there should be little difficulty for the reader, who has been given the right line of approach, and who has at his disposal a large number of commentaries, some of which ascribe to the poem depths of significance which its author has modestly disclaimed. The quickest means of reaching its meaning is probably to listen to a reading by someone who is familiar with the work, or better still, to hear Eliot's own recorded reading, made for the Library of Congress.

The form of the poem has received a good deal of attention: it is divided into five movements, and each movement has a certain completeness in itself. The musical analogy has been much stressed by critics, the different recurring themes of drought and rain, sterility and violation, ruin and social trivialities being compared with musical themes. Whilst the analogy is a useful one, it should be used with caution. It may help to suggest to the reader the kind of attention he should give, and the kind of design he should look for, but it must not be pressed further.

Nor should the poem be read as a vision of despair. It has been called Eliot's *Inferno*, but even in the *Inferno* there are gleams which recall another world. Here the vision of beauty and love is not completely shut out:

> Yet when we came back, late, from the Hyacinth garden
> Your arms full, and your hair wet, I could not
> Speak, and my eyes failed, I was neither
> Living nor dead, and I knew nothing.
> Looking into the heart of light, the silence.
> *Oed' und leer das Meer.*

Again, in the final movement, in 'the awful daring of a moment's surrender Which an age of prudence can never retract' and in the picture of guided happiness:

> The boat responded
> Gaily, to the hand expert with sail and oar
> The sea was calm, your heart would have responded
> Gaily. . . .

there is a momentary escape from the kingdoms of sterility and drought. Moreover, though the world depicted is one of disorder and decay, the poem contains within itself a subtle and implicit order which makes the vision bearable, if only just bearable. It has several times been pointed out that those recurrent images which are repeated throughout the poem 'release markedly different shades of feeling according to their special contexts'. The subtle variation between the different images of the river, for instance, or the fading of Philomel to a mere entablature in the second movement, contrasted with the violent emphasis of the third movement upon the seduction of the typist, implies some order, some principle of organization within this apparently haphazard scheme of things. The repetition with modifications of the same image cannot yield any *statement* to set against the many gestures of weariness, confusion and despair; perhaps their pattern is as arbitrary as that of the suits of a pack of cards, and indeed the symbols of the Tarot pack are in the first section identified with most of the leading symbols of the poem. Yet arbitrary as the pack of cards may be, its conventions are orderly.

As the vision of the Hyacinth girl conferred eternity upon a moment so, at the end of 'The Waste Land', there is a strange sense of expectancy, of quiet, which recalls Cleopatra's line:

> My desolation does begin to make
> A better life.

Nothing explicit warrants this feeling, except possibly the mysterious Sanscrit benediction, but it can be felt through the rhythm, which becomes stronger, more emphatic, as though a pulse were beginning to beat after the hurried staccato movement of the 'nightmare' passage at the beginning of the last movement. The words of the thunder, 'give, sympathize, control', have been fulfilled for the reader in the poem itself. The sincerity and penetration with which it renders the vision of desolation, console and demand response; whilst the power to project such a vision in the form of words, to objectify and realize it, implies the highest measure of control.

If it is not his greatest poem, 'The Waste Land' is certainly Eliot's most influential poem. The generation which grew up in the later nineteen-twenties took it to themselves, absorbed it so that it became part of their habit of mind. As Auden said in his verses for Eliot's sixtieth birthday:

> it was you
> Who, not speechless with shock but finding the right
> Language for thirst and fear, did most to
> Prevent a panic.

Moreover, the depth and violence of the contrasts in the poems, the sense that the poet is wrestling with the problems of his outer and inner world is stronger here than in the later poetry. Even in the *Four Quartets* we do not feel that 'Spinoza and the smell of the cooking' (to use Eliot's formula) have been brought into relation with each other. It is the smell of the cooking that tends to disappear. The later poems are concerned more exclusively with inner experience.

III. LATER POETRY

'The Hollow Men' (1925) marks the sharpest break in Eliot's poetry; it may be looked on as a kind of prologue or ante-chamber to 'Ash Wednesday' (1930). They have in common a new kind of image, a new kind of rhythm, and a new mood.

The world depicted in 'The Hollow Men' is a grey, phantasmal country, featureless and nameless—'death's dream kingdom'. The London of 'The Waste Land' had been as vividly realized as Baudelaire's Paris, but now the outer world is left behind. Some lines from *Four Quartets* seem best to sum up the experience conveyed in 'The Hollow Men', and its relation to 'The Waste Land':

> The strained time-ridden faces
> Distracted from distraction by distraction
> Filled with fancies and empty of meaning
> Tumid apathy with no concentration
> Men and bits of paper, whirled by the cold wind
> That blows before and after time. . . .
> Driven on the wind that sweeps the gloomy hills of London,
> Hampstead and Clerkenwell, Campden and Putney,
> Highgate, Primrose and Ludgate. Not here
> Not here the darkness, in this twittering world.
>
> Descend lower, descend only
> Into the world of perpetual solitude,
> World not world, but that which is not world,

> Internal darkness, deprivation
> And destitution of all property,
> Desiccation of the world of sense,
> Evacuation of the world of fancy,
> Inoperancy of the world of spirit. . . .
>
> 'Burnt Norton', III

'The Hollow Men' marks the dead centre in Eliot's poetry: it records the experience of utter destitution where there are no forms, not even the forms of nightmare. The 'hollow men' who are also 'the stuffed men', that is, scarecrows, straw dummies, whisper together only with the voice of the wind over dry grass. This image is taken from the last movement of 'The Waste Land', the approach to the Chapel Perilous, but it is very differently used. The stone images, the 'cactus land', and the 'beach of the tumid river' on which the hollow men gather in the twilight of death's kingdom (an image taken from the *Purgatorio*, II, 100–2) are unredeemed by any vision of beauty. That has been left behind in the world of the living:

> Eyes I dare not meet in dreams
> In death's dream kingdom
> These do not appear:
> There, the eyes are
> Sunlight on a broken column
> There, is a tree swinging
> And voices are
> In the wind's singing
> More distant and more solemn
> Than a fading star.

There is a distant, barely expressed hope that the eyes, like Beatrice's '*occhi santi*', may reappear

> As the perpetual star
> Multifoliate rose
> Of death's twilight kingdom
> The hope only
> Of empty men.

but the poem ends with a broken disconnected attempt at

phrases from the Lord's Prayer and with the empty jingle of a child's nursery rhyme.

From the passages which have just been quoted it will be seen that the rhythm of 'The Hollow Men' depends on short, nerveless lines, with occasional rather haphazard rhyming. The effect conveyed is one of peculiar exhaustion, flatness, and remoteness. The voice moves in a thin and mechanical way through the repetition of phrases and of words ('death's dream kingdom', contrasted with 'death's twilight kingdom' and 'death's other kingdom'). This mood seems to be described dramatically in the speeches of Harry in *The Family Reunion*, when he recalls to Mary, and later to Agatha, some phases of his wanderings.

Compared with 'The Hollow Men', 'Ash Wednesday' shows a movement towards recovery, a turning towards life. Whereas 'The Hollow Men' would seem to be a personal poem, recording the effects of some disaster at the moment when the shock was most severe, 'Ash Wednesday' depicts re-emergence into a new and strange world, which can be described only by formal and highly stylized images, so that the effect is still rather remote. Eliot was clearly at this time most strongly under the influence of Dante's poetry. He wrote a monograph upon Dante (reprinted in his *Selected Essays*) which provides incidentally the best comment upon his own poetry. Speaking of the Divine Pageant at the end of the *Purgatorio*—the scene in which Dante for the first time re-encounters Beatrice—he says:

It belongs to the world of what I call the *high dream*, and the modern world seems capable only of the *low dream*. I arrived at accepting it, myself, only with some difficulty. There were at least two prejudices, one against Pre-Raphaelite imagery which was natural to one of my generation, and perhaps affects generations younger than mine. The other prejudice—which affects this end of the *Purgatorio* and the whole of the *Paradiso*—is the prejudice that poetry not only must be found *through* suffering but can find its material only *in* suffering. Everything else was cheerfulness, optimism, and hopefulness; and these words stood for a great deal of what one hated in the nineteenth century. It took many years to recognize that the states of improvement and beatitude which Dante describes are still further from what the world can conceive as cheerfulness, than are his states of damnation.[1]

This passage, not only directly recalls the lines from 'Ash Wednesday', IV, where the Lady is restored, a vision sheathed with white light:

> Redeem
> The time. Redeem
> The unread vision in the higher dream
> While jewelled unicorns draw by the gilded hearse

but it also points to the lines in the opening poem:

> Consequently I rejoice, having to construct something
> Upon which to rejoice;

to the image of the purgatorial stairs in 'Ash Wednesday', III (originally published under the title of 'Al Som de l'Escalina', a phrase from the speech of Arnaut Daniel) and of course to the quotation which comes almost at the end of the poem, 'In la sua voluntade è nostra pace':

> Suffer us not to mock ourselves with falsehood
> Teach us to care and not to care
> Teach us to sit still
> Even among these rocks,
> Our peace in His will. . . .

These lines embody the theme of the whole poem: 'Teach us to care and not to care' suggests the mingled impulses of regret, renunciation, and redirection of the will which are interwoven throughout the sequence. The poem is strictly formal and makes use of the traditional formulas of the Church as well as the more personal symbols drawn from Dante and from Eliot's own earlier work. Rarefied and elusive and deeply personal as it is, though its power has always been recognized, the quality of its themes and style has made it something of a connoisseur's piece among

[1] *Selected Essays*, p. 248.

Eliot's writings. About the same time as 'Ash Wednesday', Eliot wrote a number of single poems, published in the series of *Ariel Poems* or in magazines. 'The Journey of the Magi' and 'A Song for Simeon' may be compared with 'Gerontion' as dramatic lyrics presenting a picture of a whole life, seen from the end by an old man looking back and meditating upon its significance; with the difference that the significance is now found in the Incarnation. But the poems are Songs of Experience and not religious verse, in the sense that George Herbert or Henry Vaughan wrote religious verse, that is to say, the references are oblique and implicit; there are touches of irony (especially in 'The Journey of the Magi', where the petty humiliations and discomforts of the journey stick in the mind of the Old Man and seem far clearer to him than the mysterious conclusion, which he does not understand).

The most important of the Ariel Poems is 'Marina', the dramatic monologue of old King Pericles, the hero of Shakespeare's play of that name, who meditates upon the recovery of his daughter, miraculously returned from the dead, like the Lady of 'Ash Wednesday'. This poem, one of the most beautiful and moving that Eliot has written, is prefaced by a line from Seneca's *Hercules Furens*, the cry of the hero as he emerges from the darkness of Hell to the light of day:

> Quis hic locus, quae regio, quae mundi plaga?

The sense of wonder, of the gradual return of life restored to a mind numbed by sorrow is presented in images of tenderness, in a hesitant, delicate movement of the verse, which seems to capture the moment of the old king's awakening from his trance:

> What seas what shore what grey rocks and what islands
> What water lapping the bow
> And scent of pine and the woodthrush singing through the fog
> What images return
> O my daughter. . . .

What is this face, less clear and clearer
The pulse in the arm, less strong and stronger—
Given or lent? more distant than stars and nearer than the eye.

The moment of beatitude and of recognition, which is the complementary and opposite experience to that of 'The Hollow Men', is given in terms of a landscape such as we have already seen in the last poem of 'Ash Wednesday', and are to meet again in 'The Dry Salvages'—the misty coast with granite rocks and islands, which is part of the landscape of the poet's childhood. Here, in this poem, as the images of life return, the threatening shapes of what was thought to be life 'become unsubstantial' and are seen to be a form of Death. The poem transmits an extraordinarily intimate and deeply felt state of being, in accents of remote and unearthly serenity.

Two other poems rely upon Shakespeare for their background: the two entitled jointly 'Coriolan'—'Triumphal March' and 'Difficulties of a Statesman'. These brilliant ironic monologues of the new political regime are given, the first from the mob's point of view, and the second from the politician's—the unwilling politician confronted with a 'situation of great delicacy and difficulty'. In the anxious period of the early 'thirties, before Hitler had really got going, these two poems provided a remarkable forecast of the political scene as it was to unfold itself. In 'Coriolan' Eliot projected the helplessness of the statesmen and of the crowd alike, swept towards war, and conscious only dimly, and in a lost, unfocused way of what they had abandoned or betrayed. The language and rhythm of these poems shows a greater variety than the preceding ones; there are free colloquialisms, such apparently unpoetic material as the catalogue of armaments in 'Triumphal March', yet also the dramatic flexibility of the speaking voice, and occasional lines of grand and reverberating weightiness:

Stone, bronze, stone, steel, stone, oakleaves, horses' heels
Over the paving.

In these two poems the two leading speakers of Eliot's drama seem to emerge—the Hero and the Chorus. Neither is exempt from satire; neither is wholly satirically drawn. The worried politician, trying to reconcile the conflicting interests of various parties, and the humble spectators of the triumphal procession, whose 'Please will you give us a light?' is given such unexpected depths of implication by the repetition of the last word

> Light
> Light,

were to be followed by the more fully dramatic studies of *The Rock* and *Murder in the Cathedral*. Eliot set a fashion for verse drama in the middle 'thirties, which was followed by Auden, Spender, MacNeice, and others whose attempt to write drama, and political drama especially, produced some lively *vers d'occasion* but nothing that is highly likely to survive. Eliot himself eschewed political drama, though there are implications of a political kind in *The Rock* and *Murder in the Cathedral*, in the speeches of the Tempters and the Knights in particular. During this period also Eliot wrote a number of books and articles upon social and religious questions, such as *After Strange Gods* and *The Idea of a Christian Society*. His second drama, *The Family Reunion*, appeared in 1939. It is probable that in turning to the stage he was not merely working out his own bent but was putting into practice the ideas which he expressed in *The Use of Poetry and the Use of Criticism* in 1933:

The most useful poetry, socially, would be one which could cut across all the present stratifications of public taste—stratifications which are perhaps a sign of social disintegration. The ideal medium for poetry, to my mind, and the most direct means of social 'usefulness' for poetry is the theatre. In a play of Shakespeare you get several levels of significance. For the simplest auditors there is the plot, for the more thoughtful the character and conflict of character, for the more literary the words and phrasing, for the more musically sensitive the rhythm, and for auditors of more sensitiveness and understanding a meaning which reveals itself gradually.

This passage indicates those aspects of the drama which Eliot himself was likely to find most congenial, and the last phrase suggests that method of implication and gradual exploring of the full significance of an image which has been described already as one of the leading features of his style. In 'Ash Wednesday' he had further deepened his power to explore and unfold traditional liturgical symbols. His reliance upon the liturgy, the creeds, the great public affirmations is a sign of co-ordination between the public and the private worlds. In the plays he uses historic or mythological material. Finally, in his last, and by general agreement, his greatest poem, *Four Quartets*, which was worked out slowly between 1935 and 1942, he achieved both a new depth and a new clarity. This work (like 'Ash Wednesday' and 'The Waste Land') consists of a number of poems, complete in themselves, yet also forming a unity. Each single poem is divided into five movements, and each is also named from a place: Burnt Norton—an old house in Gloucestershire, at Aston-sub-Edge under the lip of the Cotswold Hills: East Coker—the Somerset village from which Eliot's family originally came: The Dry Salvages, named from three small islands off the coast of Cape Ann: and Little Gidding, a village in Huntingdonshire, where, in the early seventeenth century, Nicholas Ferrar retired with his family to live a life of ordered devotion in his 'Protestant nunnery'. It was to be known and loved by George Herbert, to give shelter to the defeated King Charles after Naseby, and to remain as perhaps the most perfect example of that exquisite blend of piety, learning, decency, and comeliness of life which distinguished the religious life of the seventeenth century at its best.

In these poems, Eliot meditates upon a wide diversity of material: his personal experiences as they have shaped themselves into a pattern; the pattern of history, including the beginning of the war and the London blitz; the difficulties of a poet and the nature of language. Such diversity is far greater than that of 'The Waste Land', yet it is as strictly organized as 'Ash Wednesday'. The method is again *solvitur ambulando*. Phrases are repeated from poem to poem: experiences which are recognizably related, if not the same, reappear in different contexts. There are numerous echoes of the early poems, which do not have the effect of repetition, but rather of older partial statements re-integrated and completed. There is a kind of finality and mastery about the work; the ease and boldness of the transitions is coupled with a manner still tentative and exploratory, especially in the first poem. By the time the last poem is finished, the symbols have been fully unfolded, and the accent is one of assurance and power. In spite of the apparent lack of progression, by the restatement and redefinition of the symbols 'a meaning reveals itself gradually' which is then seen to have been latent, though unrecognized, in the earlier parts. This particular use of implication is assisted by various formal devices, some of which are in the nature of scaffolding and are relatively unimportant. For instance, each of the poems is concerned with one of the four elements—'Burnt Norton' with air, 'East Coker' with earth, 'The Dry Salvages' with water and 'Little Gidding' with fire. The four elements are brought together at the beginning of the second movement of 'Little Gidding', where they are seen to be symbols of multiple meaning. The water and fire are not only those of the raids on London—firemen's or bomber's elements—they are the water of baptism and the fire of purgatory, the water which is a symbol of natural life (as in 'The Waste Land') and the fire which is a symbol both of destruction and of renewal. In medieval interpretations of poetry, each statement could have three, four or sometimes even seven meanings—Dante for instance offers the interpretations of his own poems in this way in the *Vita Nuova*. Each of Eliot's poems moves upon several planes simultaneously, and can be both topical and timeless in its implications. Commentaries upon the meaning of the *Four Quartets* are almost as plentiful as

commentaries upon 'The Waste Land', and almost as diver-
gent; but the best of all has been provided by Eliot himself:

> . . . Trying to learn to use words, and every attempt
> Is a wholly new start, and a different kind of failure
> Because one has only learnt to get the better of words,
> For the thing one no longer has to say, or the way in which
> One is no longer disposed to say it. . . .
>
> Home is where one starts from. As we grow older
> The world becomes stranger, the pattern more complicated
> Of dead and living. Not the intense moment
> Isolated, with no before and after,
> But a lifetime burning in every moment,
> And not the life of one man only
> But of old stones that cannot be deciphered. . . .
>
> 'East Coker', V

> It seems, as one becomes older,
> That the past has another pattern, and ceases to be a mere
>   sequence—. . . .
> The moments of happiness—not the sense of well being,
> Fruition, fulfilment, security or affection,
> Or even a very good dinner, but the sudden illumination—
> We had the experience but missed the meaning,
> And approach to the meaning restores the experience
> In a different form, beyond any meaning
> We can assign to happiness.
>
> 'The Dry Salvages', II

> We shall not cease from exploration
> And the end of our exploring
> Will be to arrive where we started
> And know the place for the first time.
>
> 'Little Gidding', V

'The intense moment' (which is also called 'the moment
of the rose' and 'the moment of the yew tree') had been
present in 'The Waste Land' as part of an emerging but still
implicit order; in all the subsequent poetry, as remembered
experience only to be recovered through 'approach to the
meaning'. The struggle to renounce 'the infirm glory of

the positive hour' without denying its glory creates the tension of 'Ash Wednesday'. By these moments only we have existed, Eliot says in 'The Waste Land'. In *The Family Reunion* Agatha looks back to the moment when

> I only looked through the little door
> When the sun was shining on the rose-garden

yet in a sense she no longer lives by it, and has even rejected it.

> There are hours when there seems to be no past or future,
> Only a present moment of pointed light
> When you want to burn. When you stretch out your hand
> To the flames. They only come once,
> Thank God, that kind. Perhaps there is another kind,
> I believe, across a whole Thibet of broken stones,
> That lie, fang up, a lifetime's march.

However different the experience in these different contexts, it is the same *quality* of experience that is presented in each; and it is the reconciliation of these moments of illumination with the pattern of daily living which is the theme of the later works in general and of the *Four Quartets* in particular:

> I can only say, *there* we have been; but I cannot say where
> And I cannot say, how long, for that is to place it in time.
> 'Burnt Norton', II

'The point of the intersection of the timeless with time' is the theme of the dramas, and is stated most explicitly in the choruses to *The Rock*. Throughout Eliot's poetry these words re-echo, but not with the meanings they would have in prose or in philosophic discourse. The words are there to be explored, as in the passage upon different sorts of time in the first movement of 'The Dry Salvages' or the passage from the second movement quoted above, or that in the fifth movement, which concludes:

> For most of us, there is only the unattended
> Moment, the moment in and out of time,

The distraction fit, lost in a shaft of sunlight. . . .
>   These are only hints and guesses,
Hints followed by guesses; and the rest
Is prayer, observance, discipline, thought and action.
The hint half guessed, the gift half understood, is Incarnation.

What Eliot is trying to say cannot be paraphrased, reduced to a prose equivalent, or made into a message. For it is in the relationship of all the different fields of experience that are brought together in the poem that its full significance lies and these different fields of experience cannot be related by any instrument less delicate, fine, and complex than Eliot's own language. The variety of styles in *Four Quartets* ranges from epigrammatic brilliance to such beautiful lyric interludes as the sestines of 'The Dry Salvages', or the fourth movement of 'Little Gidding', in which the nature of fire is finally defined as the flame of that Third Person of the Trinity to Whom Love is appropriated as His title:

> Who then devised the torment? Love.
> Love is the unfamiliar name
> Behind the hands that wove
> The intolerable shirt of flame
> Which human power cannot remove.
> We only live, only suspire
> Consumed by either fire or fire.

In this use of a very simple and elemental symbol—which had moreover been one of the leading symbols of his own earlier poetry—Eliot seems to provide that satisfying and perfected embodiment of a long-sought truth which gives at once the impression of recognition and of discovery. Eliot himself has said elsewhere: 'A man who is capable of experience finds himself in a different world in every decade of his life; as he sees it with different eyes. the material of his art is continually renewed.' In his essay on 'Tradition and the Individual Talent', he observed that the production of a new work of art makes 'something happen simultaneously to all the works of art that preceded it. The existing monuments form an ideal order among themselves which is modified by the introduction of the new (the really new) work of art among them'. Whether or not this is true of European literature as a whole it is certainly true of Eliot's own work, which forms a closely related whole. The later work has modified, illuminated, and developed the significance of the earlier work: the strict sense of pattern which can be felt in *Four Quartets* can also be felt throughout the body of the poetry. 'East Coker' opens with the motto of Mary Stuart reversed 'In my beginning is my end' and concludes with the motto itself: 'In my end is my beginning'. In the 'contrapuntal' juxtaposition of themes, the use of implication and irony, Eliot controlled and related an unusually wide range of experience; and by the precision and conscious artistry of his style he was able to subdue and unify it. Towards the end of the last poem in *Four Quartets* he writes:

> And every phrase
> And sentence that is right (where every word is at home,
> Taking its place to support the others,
> The word neither diffident nor ostentatious,
> An easy commerce of the old and the new,
> The common word exact without vulgarity,
> The formal word precise but not pedantic,
> Then complete consort dancing together)
> Every phrase and every sentence is an end and a beginning,
> Every poem an epitaph.

Such a trained and disciplined way of writing is not common in English; and Eliot might have given the impression, in his less happy moments, of keeping too tight a rein. But in these later poems the commerce of old and new is indeed more easy and familiar; the transitions subtler and more gracious; so that such bold modifications of language as appear in describing the last of the Four Seasons in accents of the Fourth Evangelist become perfectly natural:

> Midwinter spring is its own season
> Sempiternal though sodden towards sundown,
> Suspended in time, between pole and tropic.

> When the short day is brightest, with frost and fire,
> The brief sun flames the ice, on pond and ditches,
> In a windless cold that is the heart's heat,
> Reflecting in a watery mirror
> A glare that is blindness in the early afternoon.

This landscape, at once the country round Little Gidding, and that landscape of the heart where the flames reappear after the long march across a whole Thibet of broken stones recalls, with the matter-of-fact conclusion about 'the early afternoon', that the poet is talking of a physical journey, though the spring he sees—the hedgerow blanched with snow as with blossom—is 'not in time's covenant'. This use of everyday things to mirror the sublime, as well as the formal ordering of the whole poem, is reminiscent of Dante in a deeper, though less obvious, way than the structure of 'Ash Wednesday'. Eliot uses his personal symbols to give that kind of relationship between one realm of discourse and another, which in Dante is provided both by the formal structure of the journey and also by the Thomistic structure of belief. Very rarely in the poems does Eliot make use of religious terminology, although anyone acquainted with devotional writing will recognize the background of such passages as that on the virtue of detachment ('Little Gidding', III) or the dark night of the soul ('East Coker', III), which is also a description of how things felt at the beginning of the war:

> O dark dark dark. They all go into the dark,
> The vacant interstellar spaces, the vacant into the vacant. . . .
>   As in a theatre,
> The lights are extinguished, for the scene to be changed
> With a hollow rumble of wings, with a movement of darkness
>   on darkness,
> And we know that the hills and the trees, the distant panorama,
> And the bold imposing façade are all being rolled away. . . .

The autobiographical passage in which the poet encounters the shade of the dead master at the end of a night's fire-watching is written in a modified *terza rima*, and the shade is more like Dante's than anyone else's. Here surely Eliot is speaking directly in the ironic account of 'the gifts reserved for age'. But the 'I' of the poem is perhaps no more to be identified with the poet speaking in his own person than are the passages in the first person in 'The Waste Land', spoken through the lips of Tiresias. The speakers in the early dramatic monologues were often subjected to implicit satire. In 'The Hollow Men' the 'I' has become a 'we'—for in the sheer pain of that poem the sense of personality has lapsed. Eliot's growing interest in the drama had been exercised upon material very similar to that which is the basis of *Four Quartets*. Several rather severe warnings have in any case been issued by Eliot against the personal interpretation of his writing. 'Honest criticism and sensitive appreciation is directed not upon the poet but the poetry', he observed in 'Tradition and the Individual Talent', and, a little later, 'Poetry is not a turning loose of emotion but an escape from emotion; it is not the expression of personality but an escape from personality. But of course only those who have personality and emotions know what it is to want to escape from these things.'

Yet *Four Quartets* remains a poem of inner experience. The house of Burnt Norton is empty and deserted, and only the vision of children seen in the garden suggests the possible existence of other human forms. In 'East Coker' the ghosts of the village merrymakers are seen dancing in a field at midnight: in 'The Dry Salvages', the fishermen setting and hauling, the travellers and the women

> who have seen their sons or husbands
> Setting forth and not returning

are more substantial: and in the final movement appears Eliot's old enemy, the Fortune Teller, dealer in past and future. 'Little Gidding' is filled with a sense of historic characters—Milton, Charles I, the Ferrars, Julian of Norwich whose words are quoted. The 'familiar compound ghost' who appears at the end of the air raid speaks only when the poet, 'assuming a double part', hails him; his words are mordant, sympathetic, instructive; the accent by no means unfamiliar; the effect at once of an echo and a messenger.

IV. THE DRAMATIST

Eliot's interest in the drama long preceded his experiments in dramatic form, and so his early essays on dramatic theory can be applied only with some caution to the consideration of his plays. But we have Eliot's own word that he had from the first wished to write plays, as well as the fragmentary *Sweeney Agonistes* by way of witness.

The essays on 'Rhetoric and Poetic Drama', 'Four Elizabethan Dramatists', and the 'Dialogue on Dramatic Poetry' which are all reprinted in Eliot's *Selected Essays*, were written during the 'twenties. In the first of these essays, which should be taken in conjunction with the essay on Ben Jonson, Eliot is concerned to defend rhetoric, and the 'artificial' style in drama. Jonson's rhetoric is

the careful precise filling in of a strong and simple outline, and at no point does it overflow the outline . . . there is a definite artistic emotion which demands expression at that length.

Characters are seen not in terms of individual roles, recalling figures of real life, but in 'their combination into a whole. And these figures are not personifications of passions: separately, they have not even that reality, they are constituents'. He might be describing the Tempters and the Knights of his first play, *Murder in the Cathedral*, or the uncles and aunts who form the chorus of *The Family Reunion*. Eliot sees Jonson as the follower of Marlowe, whose tragic 'farce' he succeeds with 'something falling under the category of burlesque or farce'.

In the essay on 'Four Elizabethan Dramatists' Eliot defends convention and regrets only that the Elizabethans were not more consistent in their use of it. He praises the impersonal art of the ballet:

The difference between a great dancer and a merely competent dancer
is in the vital flame, the impersonal and, if you like, inhuman force which
transpires between each of the great dancer's movements. . . . No artist
produces great art by a deliberate attempt to express his personality. He
expresses his personality indirectly through concentrating upon a task
which is a task in the same sense as the making of an efficient engine or
the turning of a jug or table leg.

In 'A Dialogue of Dramatic Poetry' Eliot again suggests that
drama should approximate to the formality of the ballet,
that verse drama is preferable to prose because 'if we want
to express the permanent and the universal we tend to
express ourselves in verse'. Poetry and drama are not
separable elements in such a play. The most successful of
Elizabethan dramatists are the most successful poets.

Eliot's own attempt to create a new drama began with
the rhythms of the music hall. The jazz songs in *Sweeney
Agonistes*, the simple caricatures who form the *dramatis
personæ* and the lurid story of murder combine into a tragic
farce.

The world of *Sweeney Agonistes* is rather like the world
of Graham Greene's early novels or Pinter's latest plays.
The gangsters, toughs, prostitutes, and dumb business men
are all pursued by hidden fear. This fear is suggested by the
ominous pounding rhythms, and the heavy repetitions and
echoes. The movement is a very simple echoing chime of
two or three voices. It starts:

> *Dusty*. How about Pereira?
> *Doris*.   What about Pereira?
>   I don't care.
> *Dusty*.   You don't care!
>   Who pays the rent?
> *Doris*.   Yes he pays the rent
> *Dusty*. Well some men don't and some men do
>   Some men don't and you know who
> *Doris*. You can have Pereira
> *Dusty*.   What about Pereira?

> *Doris.* He's no gentleman, Pereira:
>   You can't trust him!
> *Dusty.* Well that's true.

The sinister echoes are continued when Doris cuts the cards and draws the coffin (two of spades) and when Sweeney later breaks into the party with his story of the man who 'did a girl in' and kept her body in a bath.

> Nobody came
> And nobody went
> But he took in the milk and he paid the rent.

The play ends with a nightmare chorus in a rapid triple rhythm:

When you're alone in the middle of the night and you wake in a sweat and a hell of a fright. . . .

and by a slow crescendo of knocks upon the door, which presumably heralds the arrival of the dangerous Pereira.[1]

This little fragment could never have been extended into a play of any length: the rhythm is too violent and the caricature too broad. But it is the first work to introduce Eliot's dramatic style: a very free, heavily stressed irregular verse, with emphatic rhymes and an almost unvaried accent of ominous foreboding. The piece is prefaced by the words of Orestes: 'You don't see them, you don't—but I see them: they are hunting me down, I must move on.'

Eliot has said that there is nothing more dramatic than a ghost and all his plays have a potent flavour of the supernatural. His first piece of dramatic writing, a pageant called *The Rock*, was written for the Building Fund of London diocese. The choruses alone are reprinted in his *Collected Poems* and, whilst they are of interest as technical exercises, their chief significance is to show how wide the difference is between an adequate statement of 'Eliot's philosophical themes' and his genuine poetry. These choruses are neces-

[1] An unpublished final scene was given at the Globe Theatre on 13 June 1965, in a programme entitled *Homage to T. S. Eliot.*

sarily very much more simplified in rhythm and in language than his lyric poetry. They are designed to fulfil that social function of drama which he described in *The Use of Poetry and the Use of Criticism* (see p. 26). The whole work is built on the theme of religion and society. There are a few epigrammatic lines, satiric and admonitory:

> In the land of lobelias and tennis flannels
> The rabbit shall burrow and the thorn revisit,
> The nettle shall flourish on the gravel court,
> And the wind shall say 'Here were decent godless people;
> Their only monument the asphalt road
> And a thousand lost golf balls.'

This is the world of 'Coriolan', with the chorus of unemployed as background: the world of the slump and of the rise of the dictatorships in Europe. *The Rock* is frankly propaganda, and has the merits and limits of propaganda. The seventh chorus, 'In the beginning God created the world', contains in an early form some of the themes of *Four Quartets*; and the influence of Biblical rhythms, especially those parts of the Bible which form part of the public services of the Church, anticipates the use of these rhythms in the later plays.

Murder in the Cathedral (1935), *The Family Reunion* (1939), and *The Cocktail Party* (1950), form a closely related group; all retain something of the pageant, or the ballet, and are built on a contrast between the Hero and the Chorus, between the man who sees and the rest who are blind. Eliot is a dramatist in a very special and limited sense; but he recognized and used his limitations, so that his particular form of drama, though very restricted, is coherent, self-consistent and extremely actable. Like the plays of Ben Jonson, these dramas are two-dimensional but not superficial. They are plays of the surface, but the implications go far below the surface. The characters exist only in relation to each other: they fit in with each other and are constituent parts, distorted to scale, of the main theme. The action is of the slightest. A single moment of choice, the Kierke-

gaardian choice, is set before the main character; the rest
of the play leads up to and leads away from this moment.
There are no sub-plots, minor interests, or digressions. The
moment of choice is the same for all. There is often actual
repetition from one of these plays to another. As Eliot
observed in *Four Quartets:*

> You say I am repeating
> Something I have said before. I shall say it again.
> 'East Coker', III

The main theme is the relation of 'the moment in time'
to 'the moment out of time'—the moment of decision for
Thomas of Canterbury, the moment of recognition for
Harry Monchensey, the moment of blind choice for Celia.
In all three plays the central character has literally to choose
between life and death—their own deaths for Thomas and
Celia. Harry, the hero of *The Family Reunion*, who is based
on the Orestes figure which had haunted Eliot so long,
makes the choice that kills his mother, and goes forward to
an unknown future. The choice lies between two kinds of
action; the result is in each case a resolution of the dilemma.
These plays are not tragedies; they are the kinds of plays
that are written when the tragic experience—necessarily a
temporary, though an inevitable, state for each individual—
has been left behind. Eliot's tragedy, had he written one,
would have belonged to the period of 'The Hollow Men'.

The plays reflect, then, in simplified but none the less
genuine form, the same experience as *Four Quartets*,
scored for brass rather than strings. *Murder in the Cathedral*
is quite popular: *The Family Reunion*, which would appear
to be too personal, too imperfectly projected (to contain, in
short, the kind of difficulties which Eliot attributed to
Hamlet), does in fact act extremely well. *The Cocktail Party*
is technically the most developed of the three: in this
play, Eliot seems to have succeeded in finding the appro-
priate formula (the 'objective correlative', to use his own
phrase) for which he has been looking.

The assassination of Thomas à Becket is an important

event in English history: the story of the Oresteia is one of
the great myths common to Europe; the nervous break-
down, legacy of the second world war, was for some years
a determining factor of the social scene, a kind of modern
equivalent of the Black Death. Eliot has firmly rooted his
plays in these external grounds; but they are of course
essentially plays of inner experience.

> Those to whom nothing has ever happened
> Cannot understand the unimportance of events

says Harry, in *The Family Reunion*, and the Fourth Tempter
describes to Thomas a time when

> men will not hate you
> Enough to defame or to execrate you,
> But pondering the qualities that you lacked
> Will only try to find the historical fact.

The choice made by Thomas is not 'for the lifetime of
one man only'. It is seen as part of the pattern of timeless
moments: seen as such for a moment only, for as Thomas
says (echoing a line from 'Burnt Norton'):

> Human kind cannot bear very much reality.

But in the light of such moments the common man lives
out his life. In *Murder in the Cathedral*, there are three levels
of character: Thomas, who speaks with the full conscious-
ness of the Hero, the Tempters, and the Chorus of the poor
women of Canterbury, who sense the 'supernatural evil'
which is descending upon the place but who try to live out
their humble lives as unobtrusively as possible:

> We do not wish anything to happen.
> Seven years we have lived quietly,
> Succeeded in avoiding notice,
> Living and partly living.

As the 'small folk who live among small things' they are
rather unwillingly faithful, compelled to wait and bear
witness, conscious at the end of the guilt of their weakness:

Forgive us, O Lord, we acknowledge ourselves as type of the
common man,
Of the men and women who shut the door and sit by the
fire. . . .

Thomas knows that in returning he is choosing his death,
and in the scene with the Four Tempters he makes his decision to stay. He rejects the bribes of power—even the
spiritual power offered by the choice of martyrdom, which
the Fourth Tempter proffers:

The last temptation is the greatest treason:
To do the right deed for the wrong reason.

The figures of the Tempters are paralleled by the Four
Knights, who, after they have murdered Thomas, come
forward with good water-tight explanations of the neces-
sity and high-mindedness of the act. They, like the Tempters,
are given a modern colloquial idiom, and they speak in the
phrases of the modern politician. They come from the land
of lobelias and tennis flannels as well as from Aquitaine, and
the ingenuity of the final plea—that Thomas was deliberately
courting death and was therefore really responsible for what
happened ('I think, with these facts before you, you will
unhesitatingly render a verdict of Suicide while of Unsound
Mind')—does not even sound particularly far-fetched in the
light of totalitarian practices.

Satire, epigram, and social caricature alternate with the
poetic choruses in which the sense of supernatural evil is
given in verse of a free and irregular sort, based upon
Biblical rhythms, dropping sometimes into Biblical phrases,
at other times colloquial, and always highly repetitive. The
ritualistic quality of the speech, the stylized characters, and
the very limited action contrasts sharply with the complex
language (the play has long passages in prose, including a
sermon from the Archbishop). The sardonic note suggested
in the title (which might be that of a detective story) is
maintained to the last in the treatment of the Knights, who
may be reminiscent in some ways of the comic devils of

Morality plays, but are in others rather like a music-hall turn. In production, one of the Tempters carried a golf club, with which he made practice shots in the intervals of his speech.

The Family Reunion does not employ Christian terminology, nor does The Cocktail Party. This certainly does not mean that they are allegories and that as one reviewer of the latter play remarked, 'We see that the doctor *is* a priest, that his patients *are* the church. . . .' The use of a modern secular setting enables Eliot to relate his material more exactly and closely; the satire is less superficial, the integration more complete. In The Cocktail Party there is a very noticeable return to the rhythms of Sweeney Agonistes:

> *Julia.*   But how did he come here?
> *Edward.*   I don't know.
> *Julia.*   *You* don't know! And what's his name? . . . .
>   Did I hear him say his name was Riley?
> *Edward.* I don't know his name.
> *Julia.*   You don't know his *name?*
> *Edward.* I tell you I've no idea who he is
>   Or how he got here.

The bright conversation which opens this play might sound as if it were being merely too faithful to the banalities of social chatter were it not for this extremely ominous rhythm, which sounds its echoing chime all round the circle of the symmetrically grouped characters. In The Family Reunion, there is a chorus of four uncles and aunts who are used for similar purpose: they are stupid people, who do not understand what is wrong with Harry, and who are torn reluctantly away from their clubs and vicarage tea-parties to participate in the drama of the Eumenides.

The hero of The Family Reunion is haunted by a crime, and he dwells in a shadowy and terrifying world until he returns to his home. Here the guilt is lifted from him by the revelation of the past—not his own past but that of his father and mother. His father's desire to murder his

mother has been projected into a belief that he himself had
murdered his wife:

> *Harry.* Perhaps my life has only been a dream
> Dreamt through me by the minds of others. Perhaps
> I only dreamt I pushed her. . . .
> *Agatha.* So I had supposed. What of it?
> What we have written is not a story of detection,
> Of crime and punishment but of sin and expiation . . .
> It is possible
> You are the consciousness of your unhappy family,
> Its bird sent flying through the purgatorial flame. . . .

The suffering of Harry, and in a lesser degree of Mary, the
woman who had loved him but had not been noticed ('It's
just ordinary hopelessness'), and Agatha who had loved and
renounced his father, forms the core of the play. Here the
play is closest to the lyric poems, and sometimes more
moving in its simplicity. The social setting and the blind
dominating figure of the mother are there to contrast with
this core of suffering. They are not related to it. Thus the
play moves on two levels—the social and the supernatural—
like the two worlds of 'The Waste Land'.

In *The Cocktail Party* the two worlds are more closely
related. It begins with an unsuccessful party, and ends with
a successful one. In the interval the trivialities of social ex-
change have all been explored, and their implications fully
brought to light. The four main characters have reached
three several solutions; the solution of work and social
success; the solution of accepting the limits of 'the human
condition' and maintaining the common routine, learning to
avoid excessive expectation; and the other solution of a
difficult vocation and a violent death.

The minor characters, who had at first seemed so tiresome
—the interfering old woman, the helpful man of the world
—turn out to be in benevolent league with the doctor who
effects the cures, and all work together for good.

In a sense these plays are not at all realistic. It has been
said Agatha would not be likely to be elected as the principal

of a women's college, but I do not think anyone who was would fit in very comfortably to *The Family Reunion*. It has been said that Celia would not be sent straight out to a difficult country by any religious order, but her sudden exit and her violent death (which some critics, ignorant of the New Guinea martyrs, found excessively horrible) are not to be read on the level of 'the historical fact'. There are on the other hand some scenes of quite excruciating realism, such as the quarrel between Lavinia and Edward, a full-length study of the scene suggested in 'The Waste Land', II. But this is a scene which has internal significance: it is not a mere event. There is a good deal of that mordant humour which is sometimes taken amiss by inattentive readers—a tone of mock dignity and assumed gravity which Sir Henry Harcourt-Reilly shares with Agatha, and the First Priest of *Murder in the Cathedral*. It is a tone which belongs to Eliot himself:

> *Julia.* Oh, Henry!
> Lavinia is much more observant than you think.
> I believe, Henry, if I may put it vulgarly,
> That Lavina has forced you to a show down.
> *Henry.* You state the position correctly, Julia.

The epigrammatic comments recall the earliest poems. The central scene, that in which Celia states her case and makes her choice, belongs to a different mode. But this scene reflects back upon her earlier scene with Edward, her lover. In this play the past is altered by the present, and a technique of retrospective illumination enables even the frivolities of the opening lines to be recalled quite naturally at the close.

After *The Cocktail Party*, Eliot's main dramatic impulse spent itself, although in the following decade *The Confidential Clerk* (1954) and *The Elder Statesman* (1958), two lectures, *Poetry and Drama*(1951) and *The Three Voices of Poetry* (1953) extend his theory and practice of drama. The first lecture treats of the nature of dramatic writing, and of the relation between author and audience. Eliot thinks that 'the chief effect of style and rhythm in dramatic speech, whether in prose or verse, should be unconscious'; therefore there should be no disturbing transitions from one to the other:

> We should aim at a form of verse in which everything can be said that has to be said .... but if our verse is to have so wide a range that it can say anything that has to be said, it follows that it will not be 'poetry' all the time. It will only be 'poetry' when the dramatic situation has reached such a point of intensity that poetry becomes the natural utterance, because then it is the only language in which the emotions can be expressed at all.

In the second part of the lecture, Eliot describes his own experiments, the search for a form which should establish communications between the three collaborators in dramatic art—author, actors and audience:

> In the theatre, the problem of communication presents itself immediately. You are aiming to write lines which will have an immediate effect upon an unknown and unprepared audience, to be interpreted to that audience by unknown actors, rehearsed by an unknown producer.

Eliot makes it clear that he is not satisfied with any of his own experiments, and critically examines their shortcomings. Yet he captured an audience not confined to poetry-readers: both *The Cocktail Party* and *The Confidential Clerk* succeeded in the West End and on Broadway. In *The Three Voices of Poetry*, Eliot notes the slight shock thereby produced amongst those of his admirers who prefer to be among the sweet, selected few:

> It may be that from the beginning I aspired unconsciously to the theatre or as the critics might say, with more asperity, to Shaftesbury Avenue.

The three voices of poetry, as distinguished by Eliot, are that of the poet talking to himself: that of the poet talking to an audience: and that of the poet speaking through another character—or meditative, rhetorical and dramatic poetry. The comparative simplicity and directness of vocabulary,

syntax and content which he demands for the third voice
are certainly exemplified in his own work. The story of *The
Confidential Clerk* may be based on the *Ion*, but at a London
theatre I have sat behind what appeared to be the Mothers'
Meeting of some suburban church, and heard them com-
mend Act III as being 'almost like a whodunit'. Eliot would
probably have approved: the central theme of the drama,
which seems to be a search for identity, the hero's need to
establish a true self, is clothed in a fantastic tale of mistaken
identity, involving three babies (one of them, like Betsy
Trotwood Copperfield, not being forthcoming), designed to
appeal to simple tastes. The moments of poetry in this play
are very few; for the most part it is merely verse. Eliot sacri-
ficed the finer qualities of his writing to the needs of communication. One moment of poetry occurs when the hero
and his supposed father approach each other through their
common experience as frustrated artists: another is that in
which the hero and a young woman are led by the power of
music to that enkindled sympathy in which mind begins to
play in and out of mind. But the moment of inspiration and
the moment of love are alike renounced at the end of the
play, in a scene where all the characters get their wishes, only
to find that the fulfilment of a wish, since choice means
elimination, involves a kind of death as well as a rebirth. The
Cumean Sybil from Teddington who effects this is the hero's
long-lost mother: but she has deliberately forfeited her claim
to him, and he in turn now renounces all relationships:

> Let my mother rest in peace. As for a father—
> I have the idea of a father
> It's only just come to me. I should like a father
> Whom I had never known and couldn't know now,
> Because he would have died before I was born
> Or before I could remember: whom I could get to know
> Only by reports, by documents.

Perhaps some light is cast upon this Father when the former
confidential clerk says to the hero, whom he has taken under

his protection, and who replaces his own dead son, 'You'll
be thinking of reading for orders'. For Colby, like Celia, has
awakened to his vocation.

Perhaps also it is not a coincidence that there are echoes
of the two climaxes of this play in *The Three Voices of Poetry*
—especially in view of Eliot's determination to say in that
lecture something which he had *not* said before. Sir Claude
describes the 'secret moment' of the artist:

> That state of utter exhaustion and peace
> Which comes in dying to give something life. . . .

and in the lecture Eliot describes the satisfactory imposition
of form upon the psychic material which has struggled to
find it, in terms significantly new (compare p. 50) :

a moment of utter exhaustion, of appeasement, of absolution and of
something very near annihilation which is in itself indescribable.

Yet a poem is handed over to the unknown audience to
shape and reform for themselves, and this

seems to me the consummation of the process begun in solitude without
thought of the audience, the long process of gestation of the poem,
because it marks the final separation of the poem from the author. Let
the author rest in peace.

If a classical model is to be found for *The Elder Statesman*,
Oedipus at Colonus would serve. Hiding private failure
behind public success, the hero learns to live with his
ghosts—himself little more than a ghost. Cherished by his
Antigone, rejected by his son, he dies under a beech tree,
having exorcised the shadows of moral turpitude—inward
fears, though outwardly represented by two figures from
his past.

This work stands to ordinary plays rather as oratorio to
opera: it lacks the dimension of outward action. The
language has that sententious finality usually associated with
a chorus. Exploration of the connection between private
and public worlds may justify the dramatic form: the only

concession to a popular audience is a variation on the comic landlady. This is an attempt to transpose themes from poetry of the first voice into poetry of the third voice. As a perceptive critic observed, it is more effective when read than when acted; a personal note of confession and of valediction is heard in the last lines:

> Age and decrepitude can have no terrors for me,
> Loss and vicissitude cannot appal me,
> Not even death can dismay or amaze me,
> Fixed in the certainty of love unchanging.

From the late nineteen-fifties, a revival of drama has paradoxically produced the most vigorous writing of the decade by exploiting the physical conditions of the living theatre, using flat writing as part of a collaborative production. However far removed from Eliot's own drama, Beckett, Osborne, Pinter, and their contemporaries are exploring possibilities which he as a critic was the first to point out. In *The Birthday Party*, Pinter by the very title resembles Eliot: this comedy of menace, in which the hero is kidnapped by a pair of diabolic Guardians, seems like a shadow-image of Eliot's play of redemption. But unlike Eliot's work, it has little validity on the written page, and exists for production.

V. THE CRITIC AND MAN OF LETTERS

Had he not become the most famous poet of his time, Eliot would have been known as its most distinguished critic. This statement must be qualified by adding that it is really impossible to distinguish the poet and the critic; for his criticism springs from his poetic sensibility and his poetry is best explained in terms of his criticism. Among English critics the most memorable are those who have also been creative artists—Philip Sidney, Ben Jonson, Dryden, Samuel Johnson, Coleridge, and Arnold. Indeed Eliot once ventured upon the statement that he thought 'the *only* critics worth reading were the critics who practised and practised well, the art of which they wrote'. This extreme view he did not attempt seriously to sustain; but his definition of the function of criticism, as of the perfect critic, assumes that

the two directions of sensibility are complementary; and as sensibility is rare, unpopular and desirable, it is to be expected that the critic and the creative artist should frequently be the same person.

'The Perfect Critic' (*The Sacred Wood*, 1920)

Eliot's conception of the true critic is that he should be impersonal, instructed and without either the unfulfilled creative impulses which make some criticism an imperfect form of creation or the desire to use literature as a substitute for other things, e.g. for religion. The first type of 'imperfect critic' is exhibited by Eliot in the person of Arthur Symons: 'the reading sometimes fecundates his emotions to produce something new which is not criticism, but is not the expulsion, the ejection, the birth of creativeness'. The second type of 'imperfect critic' is discerned in Matthew Arnold. 'The total effect of Arnold's philosophy is to set up Culture in the place of Religion and to leave Religion to be laid waste by the anarchy of feeling.'

The task of the critic is defined in the words of Rémy de Gourmont: 'Eriger en lois ses impressions personelles, c'est le grand effort d'un homme s'il est sincère.' Taking for granted that the critic is a man of natural sensibility, the impressions of his reading will 'tend to become articulate in a generalized statement of literary beauty' since 'perceptions do not, in a really appreciative mind, accumulate as a mass, but form themselves into a structure; and criticism is the statement in language of this structure: it is a development of sensibility'.

The work of a good critic will therefore appear cold and impersonal to the reader in search of a stimulus; for it is not the business of the critic to stimulate but to put the reader in possession of the necessary facts—not, of course, simply external facts, but the presentation of the work of art itself, e.g. by commentary or reading, which is one of the subtlest forms of interpretation. 'But in matters of great importance the critic must not coerce and he must not make judgements of better and worse. He must simply elucidate; the reader will form the correct judgement for himself.'

In 'Tradition and the Individual Talent', the process of poetic creation itself is also described as 'a continual self-sacrifice, a continual extinction of personality', and the poet is compared with a catalytic agent, whose part in a chemical reaction is simply to induce the reaction and not to participate. Later, this moment of creation is redefined (see p. 47).

It follows that the emotional critic is almost necessarily a bad critic; and while scholars or dealers in facts cannot corrupt, 'the real corruptors are those who supply opinion or fancy; and Goethe and Coleridge are not guiltless—for what is Coleridge's *Hamlet*: is it an honest inquiry as far as the data permit, or is it an attempt to present Coleridge in an attractive costume?'

Reserve, self-suppression and the search for structural principles by submission to experience are not only the virtues of the critic, they are the most striking features of Eliot's early poetry. His method of juxtaposing two scenes, or two worlds, and leaving them to make their comment on each other, his reliance upon implication and what he himself called the contrapuntal method has been described above (see p. 12): it is the exact equivalent of his advocacy of the Socratic, or maieutic method, in criticism. The ironic concentration of his poetic style is likewise paralleled by the terse, epigrammatic and almost equally concentrated style of his prose. He himself described it in an ironic little poem:

> How unpleasant to meet Mr. Eliot!
> With his features of clerical cut,
> And his brow so grim,
> And his mouth so prim,
> And his conversation so nicely
> Restricted to What Precisely
> And If and Perhaps and But.

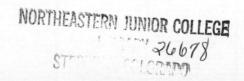

Eliot's style is indeed stripped and neutral, though not without powerful resources of tone and inflexion. It works much in terms of negatives, qualifications and restrictions:

> It is not so easy to see propriety in an image which divests a snake of *winter weeds.* . . .
> We are baffled by the attempt to translate the quality indicated by the dim and antiquated term wit, into the equally unsatisfactory nomenclature of our own times. . . .

Precisely this lack of a general critical terminology was responsible for much of his nervous stiffness and defensive irony, and the 'pontifical' tone for which Eliot was later to apologize. Like the poet, the critic of the early nineteen-twenties found himself in a waste land, and had little upon which he could rely in the way of equipment. Eliot was indebted principally to the French critics of the late nineteenth and early twentieth century, and perhaps also to the critical prefaces of Henry James. He was engaged upon an exploration of the principles of criticism as well as an examination in detail of the work of those poets to whom he as a poet was most particularly indebted. His general theory of literature is set forth in 'The Perfect Critic', 'Imperfect Critics', 'Tradition and the Individual Talent' and 'The Function of Criticism'. The first three appeared in *The Sacred Wood* and the last in *Selected Essays* (1932). These brief works exercised an influence out of all proportion to their scale; and the Cambridge school of criticism, as it has come to be called (without perhaps very much justification) is based largely upon the early critical writings of T. S. Eliot and of I. A. Richards, which also form the basis of the 'new criticism' in America.

Eliot's work upon individual writers was even more influential in redirecting the taste of the day. Based upon his experience as a poet, it attempted to 'reopen old communications' and 'to bring back the poet to life—the great, the perennial task of criticism'. In a definition of the two-fold function of criticism he remarked that there are two theoretical limits of criticism, at one of which we attempt to answer the question 'What is poetry?' and at the other, 'Is this a good poem?' He goes on:

No theoretical ingenuity will suffice to answer the second question because no theory can amount to much which is not founded upon a direct experience of good poetry; but on the other hand our direct experience of poetry involves a good deal of generalizing activity.

In Eliot's writings on individual poets, the precise quality of their work is shown by carefully placed and exactly chosen quotation. The quotations are made to do the critic's work, and the reader is made to work on them. They are more than happy quotations in the usual sense: frequently they constitute his main statement. In this way they recall the use of quotation in his poetry. The reader is obliged to work over these particular lines, to respond actively to them, to relate them to all his past experience of the writer under discussion. Hence the strength with which Eliot's quotations stamp themselves on the mind of the reader and the frequency with which they pass into general circulation.

His earliest critical essays, *The Sacred Wood* (1920) and *Homage to John Dryden* (1924) contained, besides the essays on general subjects, the studies of Ben Jonson, Marlowe, and Massinger, the Metaphysical Poets, Andrew Marvell and John Dryden. In these, Eliot set the fashion for a whole decade. The complex, ironic and sceptical poetry of Donne and of Marvell was very much to the taste of the age; whilst the poetry of rhetorical writers, who maintained a surface approach but implied the depths they did not directly explore, was almost equally suited to a generation which avoided all fundamental questions, denied the validity of metaphysics, and found refuge in a bright and brittle disillusionment. The Elizabethan poets and the Metaphysical poets—Donne, Herbert, Herbert of Cherbury, Marvell, and the rest—were of course amongst the strongest shaping influences upon Eliot's own poetry. His revaluation of their work indicates what he learnt from them; the famous passage about 'wit' in the essay on Andrew Marvell might have been written of his own verse:

Wit is not erudition; it is sometimes stifled by erudition, as in much of Milton. It is not cynicism, though it has a kind of toughness which may be confused with cynicism by the tender minded. It is confused with erudition because it belongs to an educated mind, rich in generations of experience, and it is confused with cynicism because it implies a constant inspection and criticism of experience. It involves, probably, a recognition, implicit in the expression of every experience, of other kinds of experience which are possible.

The contrasts with poetry of the nineteenth century, such as William Morris's 'Song of Hylas', or that between Dryden and Milton, served not only to define the quality of the poets from whom Eliot learnt so much but also to define those qualities of which he disapproved. His attitude towards Milton has become notorious; in a lecture given before the British Academy in 1947, Eliot achieved a delicate and diplomatic *démenti*, on the grounds that whilst Milton was a bad influence in the nineteen-twenties, when the need was for flexibility, variety, and experiment, he had now ceased to be a bad influence for young practitioners, who were rather in need of restraint:

It was one of our tenets that verse should have the virtues of prose, that diction should become assimilated to cultivated contemporary speech, before aspiring to the elevation of poetry. Another tenet was that the subject matter and the imagery of poetry should be extended to topics and objects related to the life of a modern man or woman: that we were to seek the non-poetic, to seek even material refractory to transmutation into poetry, and words and phrases which had not been used in poetry before. And the study of Milton could be of no help: it was only a hindrance.

We cannot in literature, any more than in the rest of life, live in a perpetual state of revolution. . . . Poetry should help not only to refine the language of the time, but to prevent it from changing too rapidly: a development of language at too great speed would be a development in the sense of a progressive deterioration, and that is our danger today.

It cannot be denied that when Eliot uttered these words, the attitude of the aged and distinguished Academicians who formed the audience was rather reminiscent of the Inquisition listening to the recantation of a dangerous and influential heretic. One of them even cried out (although the whole performance was being broadcast), 'A little louder, please!' But Eliot never recanted on the subject of the nineteenth-century poets. It is true that he edited an anthology of Kipling, with an introduction in which he paid tribute to Kipling's technical powers. But Matthew Arnold and the Pre-Raphaelites remain unreprieved.

One or two of Eliot's critical phrases have attained a popularity which, he said, was 'astonishing to their author'. The 'dissociation of sensibility' which he described as setting in with Milton and Dryden is one of them. In the later seventeenth century, the peculiar unification of thought and feeling which he discerned in Donne and Marvell was broken up:

A thought to Donne was an experience: it modified his sensibility. When a poet's mind is perfectly equipped for its work, it is constantly amalgamating disparate experience: the ordinary man's experience is irregular, fragmentary, chaotic. The latter falls in love, or reads Spinoza, and these two experiences have nothing to do with each other, or with the noise of the typewriter or the smell of cooking: in the mind of the poet these experiences are always forming new wholes.

It is the forming of new wholes, the *relating* of experience which Eliot learnt from the Elizabethans and from the metaphysicals, and this was what he particularly valued in their work. His account of the poetic experience is clearly based upon the great definition by Coleridge of the Poetic Imagination from the fourteenth chapter of *Biographia Literaria*. He quotes this passage in his essay on Andrew Marvell. The poet who is least represented in this phase of Eliot's crtiticism is Shakespeare himself. The essay on *Hamlet* is a document more revealing of Eliot's own difficulties than of Shakespeare's: it might stand, for instance, in part at least as a commentary on *Sweeney Agonistes*.

During the later nineteen-twenties Eliot published a number of essays, but the little monograph on Dante (1929) marks the next phase in his critical development. It coincides with the change in his poetic style which has been already described (see p. 20). At this time he also wrote an essay comparing Dante and Donne, to the great advantage of the former. The poetry of Dante remained the greatest single discernible influence in the writing of Eliot, and his interest in medieval literature, like his earlier interest in the seventeenth century, promoted a general taste for the period. Later contributions took the more informal mode of public lectures, in one of which, *The Frontiers of Criticism* (1956) he summed up the merits and defects of his own earlier 'workshop criticism'. In his last work, a study of George Herbert, Eliot took a point of view opposite to that of 'Tradition and the Individual Talent', for he saw Herbert's poetry as 'a personal record', and, some may feel, a record with a certain likeness to Eliot's own.

V. CONCLUSION

Eliot's death on 4 January 1965 seemed to come as the end of that long farewell which gave to his last play its deeply personal poignancy:

> He has gone too far to return to us.

In his line of traditional and civilized poetry, he has left no successor. His unique position of authority, comparable only with that of Samuel Johnson, derived from a variety of causes. In the first place, the particular consistency and coherence of his writing made it a structural whole: indeed in his later work, the interest of its place in the whole sometimes predominated over the effect of the particular part. The risk of over-determination has not always been avoided, although a constant development of theme can also be followed, the early themes of the City and the Garden giving way to those of identity and relationship, communication and solitude.

The range of Eliot's output and literary concerns also conferred authority; during the decade and a half that he edited the *Criterion*, this quarterly journal was one of the most influential literary publications of its time, and in its editorials appeared some of Eliot's best occasional writing, trenchant and invigorating. The publishing firm of which he was a director, Faber and Faber, specialized in poetry, and the work of many younger poets appeared under its imprint.

But Eliot did not enjoy the atmosphere of academies, literary societies or intellectual good causes, and some of his tastes were even unliterary. He published an extremely lively book of comic verse about cats, written originally for children, but designed to appeal to all who appreciate the naturally lawless behaviour, intellectual superiority, and strong business instincts of cats. 'Old Possum'—Pound's nickname for him—remained an elusive jester, whose taste for practical jokes was known in private, but whose peculiar (and rather American) brand of irony was liable to be misunderstood in public.

The title of one book describes him as *The Invisible Poet*. In the last few years, when his health became precarious, Eliot tended to withdraw more and more from the literary scene, yet at the same time relaxing the impersonality of his earlier position, he gradually conceded some elements of an intellectual autobiography. His mischievous confession, that the notes to 'The Waste Land' were originally supplied to fill out the bulk of a slender volume, was perhaps a half-truth combining ironic self-deflation with mockery of his more pedantic followers. But final publication of his forty-eight-year old Harvard thesis, *Knowledge and Experience in the Philosophy of F. H. Bradley*, as a 'curiosity of biographical interest' provided a new and much more extended commentary on the poem. As philosophy, the work of the man whom Bertrand Russell described as 'my best pupil at Harvard' shows little trace of Russell's influence; it is written in terminology that philosophers no longer employ and which Eliot confessed in 1964 that he was no longer able to think in—'Indeed, I do not pretend to understand it'! Originally composed only because 'Harvard had made it possible for me to go to Oxford for a year; this return at least I owed to Harvard', its sustained argument confirms that the cryptic style of Eliot's other early prose was assumed for a purpose. Parts of the Conclusion reveal something of the poet behind the philosopher: this constitutes its interest:

If you will find the mechanical anywhere, you will find it in the workings of mind; and to inspect living mind, you must look nowhere but in the world outside.

Our first step is to discover what experience is not, and why it is essentially indefinable.

The world, as we have seen, exists only as it is found in . . . experiences so mad and strange that they will be boiled away before you boil them down to one heterogeneous mass.

Now that his achievement is completed, those who have lived with Eliot's work, and felt it changing and growing while remaining a unity, can absorb its final form. The power to grow and change will remain with it, however, as it develops within the minds of its readers, at those deeper levels where 'words, after speech, reach Into the silence'.

On the red stone which commemorates Eliot at East Coker where he lies buried are carved only the words 'Remember Thomas Stearns Eliot, Poet', the dates of birth and death and the two phrases 'In my beginning is my end', and, 'In my end is my beginning'.

T. S. ELIOT

A Select Bibliography

(Place of publication London, unless stated otherwise)

Bibliography:

A BIBLIOGRAPHY, by D. Gallup (1952)
—a complete and accurate record to date, including contributions to periodicals and translations into foreign languages.

Collected Works:

ARA VOS PREC (1920). *Verse*
—a limited edition incorporating the contents of *Prufrock* (1917) and *Poems* (1919), with additional poems, including 'Gerontion'.

POEMS 1909–1925 (1925)
—incorporates the contents of *Ara Vos Prec* (1920), together with *The Waste Land* (1922) and 'The Hollow Men'.

COLLECTED POEMS 1909–1935 (1936)
—incorporates the contents of *Poems* 1909–1925, together with *Ash Wednesday* (1930), 'Ariel Poems', 'Unfinished Poems', 'Minor Poems', Choruses from *The Rock* (1934), and 'Burnt Norton'. Two volumes of selections from this collection were published: (i) *The Waste Land and Other Poems* (Sesame Books, 1940), (ii) *Later Poems* 1925–1935 (Faber Library, 1941). Both volumes were reprinted together in 1948 by Penguin Books. This Penguin edition was replaced in 1954 by an edition in cloth boards, published by Faber & Faber. The original edition was reprinted in the Faber Paper Covered Editions in 1958.

THE COMPLETE POEMS AND PLAYS; New York (1952)
—available only in the American edition.

COLLECTED PLAYS (1962).

COLLECTED POEMS 1909–1962 (1963).

Selected Works:

SELECTED ESSAYS 1917–1932 (1932; enlarged edition, omitting dates from title, 1951)
—contains essays from various sources, including a selection from *The Sacred Wood* (1920) and *For Lancelot Andrewes* (1928).

ESSAYS ANCIENT AND MODERN (1936)
—supersedes *For Lancelot Andrewes* (but omitting certain essays the author did not wish to preserve) and incorporates additional essays, including prefaces to Pascal's *Pensées* and Tennyson's *In Memoriam*. The author's choice of essays from this collection was added to the enlarged edition (1951) of *Selected Essays*.

SELECTED PROSE, ed. J. Hayward (1953)
—paperback. Reprinted 1963.

ON POETRY AND POETS (1957)
—contains essays, lectures and addresses from various sources, written and separately printed (with one exception) since the publication of the first edition, 1932, of *Selected Essays*.

SELECTED POEMS (1961).

TO CRITICIZE THE CRITIC (1965)
—lectures and essays from various periods, collected by Eliot but issued posthumously.

POEMS WRITTEN IN EARLY YOUTH (1967)
—reissue of an edition collected by John Hayward and privately printed, 1950, under the supervision of the author.

Separate Works:

PRUFROCK AND OTHER OBSERVATIONS (1917). *Verse*

EZRA POUND HIS METRIC AND POETRY; New York (1917). *Criticism*
—published anonymously.

POEMS (1919). *Verse*
—hand-printed by Leonard and Virginia Woolf at the original Hogarth Press, Richmond, Surrey.

THE SACRED WOOD: ESSAYS ON POETRY AND CRITICISM (1920). *Criticism*
—contains essays and reviews originally contributed to the *Times Literary Supplement*, the *Athenæum*, the *Egoist* (of which Eliot was assistant editor 1917–19), etc.

THE WASTE LAND; New York (1922). *Verse*
—first printed in the first number of the *Criterion* (October 1922). First English edition, 1923, hand-printed by Leonard and Virginia Woolf at the original Hogarth Press, Richmond, Surrey. Limited edition, 1962. The French version (in *Poèmes* 1910–1930, trans. P. Leyris, Paris, 1947) contains additional notes by John Hayward.

HOMAGE TO JOHN DRYDEN (1924). *Criticism*
—contains 'John Dryden', 'The Metaphysical Poets', 'Andrew Marvell'.

JOURNEY OF THE MAGI (1927). *Verse*
—No. 8 of the publisher's series of 'Ariel Poems' (single poems issued as pamphlets) to which the poet subsequently contributed 'A Song For Simeon', No. 16 (1928); 'Animula', No. 23 (1929); 'Marina', No. 29 (1930); 'Triumphal March', No. 35 (1931); 'The Cultivation of Christmas Trees', New Series (1954).

FOR LANCELOT ANDREWES—ESSAYS ON STYLE AND ORDER (1928). *Criticism*
—now permanently out of print. See under *Essays Ancient and Modern*, 1936.

DANTE (1929). *Criticism*

ASH WEDNESDAY (1930). *Verse*
—a signed and limited edition of 600 copies, published simultaneously in London and New York, preceded the ordinary edition by five days.

ANABASIS—A POEM BY ST J. PERSE WITH A TRANSLATION BY T. S. ELIOT (1930). *Translation*
—revised editions, New York, 1938, and New York, 1949.

THOUGHTS AFTER LAMBETH (1931). *Church Politics*
—a pamphlet, containing critical observations on ecclesiastical policy discussed at the Lambeth Conference.

JOHN DRYDEN: THE POET, THE DRAMATIST, THE CRITIC; New York (1932). *Criticism*

SWEENEY AGONISTES—FRAGMENTS OF AN ARISTOPHANIC MELODRAMA (1932). *Poetic Drama*

THE USE OF POETRY AND THE USE OF CRITICISM (1933). *Criticism*
—sub-titled 'Studies in the Relation of Criticism to Poetry in England', these essays were originally delivered as lectures at Harvard during the author's tenure (1932–3) of the Charles Eliot Norton Professorship of Poetry.

AFTER STRANGE GODS—A PRIMER OF MODERN HERESY (1934). *Sociology*
—the Page-Barbour Lectures at the University of Virginia, 1933. Now permanently out of print.

THE ROCK—A PAGEANT PLAY (1934). *Verse Libretto*

—['Book of Words'], 'Written for Performance at Sadler's Wells Theatre 28 May–9 June, 1934, on behalf of the Forty-Five Churches Fund of the Diocese of London'.

ELIZABETHAN ESSAYS (1934). *Criticism*

—collected essays on Elizabethan and Jacobean drama. The essay on John Marston is the only one not previously printed in book form. This essay was added to the enlarged edition (1951) of *Selected Essays*. A different selection, entitled *Essays on Elizabethan Drama*, was published as a paper-covered 'Harvest Book', New York, 1956.

MURDER IN THE CATHEDRAL (1935). *Poetic Drama*

—certain alterations were made in the second (1936), third (1937) and fourth (1938) editions. The film script (1951) contains considerable additions to the text. Edited with notes and introduction by Nevill Coghill, 1965.

THE FAMILY REUNION (1939). *Poetic Drama*

OLD POSSUM'S BOOK OF PRACTICAL CATS (1939). *Verse*

—verse-biographies of fanciful cats, written for children, and published under an intimate pseudonym originally coined by Ezra Pound.

THE IDEA OF A CHRISTIAN SOCIETY (1939). *Sociology*

THE MUSIC OF POETRY (1942). *Criticism*

—the third W. P. Ker Memorial Lecture delivered in the University of Glasgow, 24 February 1942.

THE CLASSICS AND THE MAN OF LETTERS (1942). *Criticism*

—the Presidential Address delivered to the Classical Association, 15 April 1942.

REUNION BY DESTRUCTION (1943). *Church Politics*

—'Reflections on a Scheme for Church Union in South India, addressed to the Laity.'

FOUR QUARTETS; New York (1943). *Verse*

—first English edition, 1944. Limited edition, 1961. Each of the four 'Quartets' was previously published as a separate pamphlet: 'Burnt Norton' (first printed in *Collected Poems*, 1909–1935); 'East Coker' in 1940; 'The Dry Salvages' in 1941; 'Little Gidding' in 1942. The French version ('Quatre Quattuors', trans. P. Leyris, Paris, 1950) contains notes by John Hayward.

WHAT IS A CLASSIC? (1945). *Criticism*

—an Address delivered to the Virgil Society, 16 October 1944.

MILTON (1947). *Criticism*
—the Master Mind Lecture for 1947, delivered to the British Academy.

NOTES TOWARDS THE DEFINITION OF CULTURE (1948). *Sociology*

THE COCKTAIL PARTY (1950). *Poetic Drama*
—certain alterations were made in the text of the second edition. Reprinted in paperback in 1958.

POETRY AND DRAMA; Cambridge, Mass. (1951)
—the first Theodore Spencer Memorial Lecture, delivered at Harvard, 21 November 1950. The author's most complete statement on this subject; English edition, 1951.

AN ADDRESS TO MEMBERS OF THE LONDON LIBRARY (1952)
—the Presidential Address, 1952, Limited to 500 copies.

AMERICAN LITERATURE AND THE AMERICAN LANGUAGE; St Louis (1953). *Criticism*
—a Centenary Address at Washington University, St Louis.

THE THREE VOICES OF POETRY (1953). *Criticism*
—the 11th Annual Lecture, 1953, of the National Book League.

THE CONFIDENTIAL CLERK (1954). *Poetic Drama*
—new edition, 1967.

GOETHE AS SAGE; Hamburg (1954)
—text in German and English of the lecture delivered at Hamburg on receiving the Hanseatic Goethe Prize, 1954.

THE FRONTIERS OF CRITICISM; Minneapolis (1956)
—the Gidea-Seymour Memorial Lecture at the University of Minnesota, 1956.

THE ELDER STATESMAN (1959). *Poetic Drama*

GEORGE HERBERT (1962). *Essay*
—in the present series, 'Writers and Their Work'.

KNOWLEDGE AND EXPERIENCE IN THE PHILOSOPHY OF F. H. BRADLEY (1963). *Dissertation*
—completed in 1916 'in partial fulfilment of the requirements' for the Harvard Ph.D. First published 47 years later 'only as a curiosity of biographical interest'.

Note: Eliot made contributions in prose or verse to over a hundred books or pamphlets by other writers; his contributions in prose or verse to periodicals (including numerous book-reviews, broadcast lectures, and the 'Commentaries' written for the *Criterion* during his editorship, 1922–39) number close on six hundred. The majority of these contributions have not been reprinted or collected. In addition Eliot edited and introduced *Selected Poems* by Ezra Pound (1928); *Selected Poems* by Marianne Moore (1935); *A Choice of Kipling's Verse* (1941); *A Selection of Joyce's Prose* (1942); *Literary Essays* by Ezra Pound (1953).

Some Biographical and Critical Studies:

'The Love Song of J. Alfred Prufrock', by E. Pound; *Poetry, Chicago* 10, 1917
—the first understanding criticism of Eliot's work to appear in print.

THE LAMP AND THE LUTE, by B. Dobrée; Oxford (1929)
—contains a critical essay on Eliot's early work. Second edition, 1964, with an additional essay on his last two plays.

AXEL'S CASTLE, by E. Wilson; New York (1931)
—contains the first important critical estimate of Eliot's work.

THOMAS STEARNS ELIOT, by T. MacGreevy (1931)
—a short study and the first book entirely devoted to Eliot's work.

NEW BEARINGS IN ENGLISH POETRY, by F. R. Leavis (1932)
—contains a penetrating critique.

THE CRITICAL IDEAS OF T. S. ELIOT, by A. Oras; Tartu [Dorpat] (1932)
—a comprehensive survey, in English, by an Esthonian critic.

MEN WITHOUT ART, by Wyndham Lewis (1934)
—contains a long critique by one of Eliot's earliest and most intelligent critics.

THE ACHIEVEMENT OF T. S. ELIOT, by F. O. Matthiessen (1935)
—the most comprehensive and important study of the inter-war years. Revised and enlarged edition, 1947. Supplemented in the Third Edition, 1958, by a chapter on Eliot's later work and an appreciation of Matthiessen, both by C. L. Barber.

'T. S. Eliot and Dante', by M. Praz; *Southern Review*, II, 3, 1937.

THE HARVARD ADVOCATE, CXXV, 3 (1938)
—this issue of the periodical, of which Eliot was one of the editors, 1909–10, contains tributes by such leading American poets and critics as Aiken, Blackmur, Eberhart, Macleish, Matthiessen, Stevens, Tate, Penn Warren, Carlos Williams.

THE QUEST FOR SALVATION IN AN ANCIENT AND MODERN PLAY, by
M. Bodkin (1941)
—analogizes the *Oresteia* and *The Family Reunion*.

'T. S. Eliot's Later Poetry', by F. R. Leavis; *Education and the University*, 1943.

FOUR QUARTETS REHEARSED, by R. Preston (1946)
—an essay in interpretation.

T. S. ELIOT: A STUDY OF HIS WRITINGS BY VARIOUS HANDS, ed. B. Rajan
(1947)
—contains eight critical essays (by Cleanth Brooks, E. E. Duncan Jones, H. Gardner, M. C. Bradbrook, etc.) and a bibliographical check-list.

T. S. ELIOT: A SELECTED CRITIQUE, ed. L. Unger; New York (1948)
—a useful collection from various sources (principally learned periodicals) of 31 extracts from important critical studies. Contains an extensive check-list of books and articles in English about Eliot's work up to 1948, the year in which he was awarded the Nobel Prize.

T. S. ELIOT: A SYMPOSIUM, compiled by R. March and Tambimuttu
(1948)
—a tribute to T. S. Eliot, on his 60th birthday. Contains 47 contributions, including poems, essays, and personal reminiscences.

SIX ESSAYS ON THE DEVELOPMENT OF T. S. ELIOT, by F. Wilson (1948).

THE ART OF T. S. ELIOT, by H. Gardner (1949)
—an excellent introduction to Eliot's poems and poetic dramas.

T. S. ELIOT: THE DESIGN OF HIS POETRY, by E. Drew; New York (1949)
—a Jungian interpretation. English edition, 1950.

POETRY AND BELIEF IN THE WORKS OF T. S. ELIOT, by K. Smidt; Oslo
(1949)
—English edition, revised, 1961. A study of the philosophic affiliations of Eliot's thought.

A READER'S GUIDE TO T. S. ELIOT, by G. Williamson; New York (1953).

THE EMPEROR'S CLOTHES, by K. Nott (1953)
—contains a spirited attack on Eliot's orthodoxy.

T. S. ELIOT'S POETRY AND PLAYS, by G. Smith, Jr.; Chicago (1956)
—an exhaustive study of Eliot's literary sources.

THE SHAPING SPIRIT, by A. Alvarez (1958)
—typical of the younger generation's criticism of Eliot.

T. S. ELIOT: A SYMPOSIUM, ed. N. Braybrooke (1958)
—contributed by some 50 authors in honour of Eliot's 70th birthday.

POETRY AND MORALITY: STUDIES ON THE CRITICISM OF M. ARNOLD,
    T. S. ELIOT AND F. R. LEAVIS, by V. Buckley (1959).

THE INVISIBLE POET: T. S. ELIOT, by H. Kenner (1960).

THE PLAYS OF T. S. ELIOT, by D. E. Jones (1960).

T. S. ELIOT, by L. Unger; Minneapolis, Minnesota (1961).

EXPERIENCE INTO WORDS, by D. W. Harding (1963).

SOME FIGURES BEHIND T. S. ELIOT, by H. Howarth (1965).

ENGLISH DRAMATIC FORM, by M. C. Bradbrook (1965)
—contains a chapter on Eliot's dramas.

THE MAKING OF 'THE COCKTAIL PARTY', by E. Martin Browne
—the Judith E. Wilson Lecture. Cambridge 1966. An account of the
    different versions, based on recollection and private letters and
    memoranda.

T. S. ELIOT AND THE ENGLISH POETIC TRADITION, by Helen L. Gardner
—the Byron Lecture, Nottingham, 1966.

T. S. ELIOT, THE MAN AND HIS WORK, ed. Allen Tate, 1967
—a collection of 26 essays, with some intimate personal recollections
    from members of Eliot's London literary and dramatic circle and
    other friends—I. A. Richards, Herbert Read, Stephen Spender,
    Ezra Pound, Frank Morley, E. Martin Browne, Robert Speight
    etc. Originally these essays appeared in *The Sewanee Review*.

Note: In 1965 the late John Hayward's matchless collection of the
works of T. S. Eliot passed by bequest to King's College, Cambridge.
In addition to an almost complete assemblage of printed works by
and about Eliot, the collection contains a very extensive group of his
manuscripts and typescripts. For the present those who wish to
consult unpublished material should in the first instance write to
T. S. Eliot's Literary Executrix, c/o Faber and Faber Ltd, 24 Russell
Square, London W.C.1.

INDEX TO COLLECTED ESSAYS

The title(s) in italics indicates the volume title(s)

66

*The essays marked with an asterisk in this list were added to the enlarged edition (1951) of *Selected Essays*.

WRITERS AND THEIR WORK

General Editor: GEOFFREY BULLOUGH

The first 55 issues in the Series appeared under the General Editorship of T. O. BEACHCROFT
Issues 56-169 appeared under the General Editorship of BONAMY DOBRÉE